Proverbs 1-9

Wise Up and Live

John A. Stewart

Second Printing – December 2007
Lamplighters International
St. Louis Park, Minnesota USA 55416

Lamplighters International equips churches to make disciples of Jesus Christ. The ministry publishes Christ-centered, Bible-based teaching discipleship resources and conducts discipleship seminars and conferences.

For additional information about the Lamplighters ministry resources contact:
Lamplighters International 6301 Wayzata Blvd, St. Louis Park, Minnesota USA 55416 or visit our website at www.LamplightersUSA.org.

ISBN # 978-1-931372-19-0
Order # Pro1-NK-SS

Contents

How to Use This Study

What Is Lamplighters International?

Lamplighters International is a discipleship-training ministry. The ministry provides churches, small groups, and individual Christians with Bible-based, Christ-centered discipleship resources and training (through local church seminars and workshops) and equips them to be intentional about making disciples of Jesus Christ.

How to Use a Self Study Edition

This Self-Study Edition is a self-contained discipleship-training course and an integral part of the entire Lamplighters discipleship series. The Proverbs Bible Study is comprised of five or ten lessons, depending on the format you choose (completing the study in five weeks or in ten). After completing the entire study, you'll have a greater understanding of significant portions of God's Word, with new truths to apply to your life.

How to Study a Lamplighters Lesson

A Lamplighters lesson begins with prayer, your Bible, the weekly lesson, and a sincere desire to learn more about God's Word. Throughout the study, all Scriptures are presented in bold type, and questions follow sequentially the Scripture reading. You should wait to use biblical commentaries or other reference books until after you've completed your weekly lesson and met with your class. Approaching the Bible study in this way gives you the opportunity to discover for yourself valuable insights from the Word of God.

You'll need approximately twenty to thirty minutes to complete either Part "a" or "b" of a lesson. The pastor or teacher will be available to help you find answers to the more difficult questions, if needed. Many students find it helpful to begin their study early in the week so they have enough time to meditate on the questions that require careful consideration.

Write answers in your own words in the spaces provided. Also, write the appropriate verse references with your answers, unless the question calls for a personal opinion. You'll find the answers either in the Scripture references at the end of the questions or in the passages listed at the beginning of each study.

"Do You Think" Questions

Most weekly lessons have a few *"do you think"* questions. In the first lesson, these questions are in italic type for easy identification. Make a special effort to answer the *"do you think"* questions because they're designed to help you apply God's Word to your life. Your insightful answers to these questions could be also a great source of encouragement to others in your study group.

Personal Questions

Occasionally, some of the study questions require introspection and a personal response. Answer these questions for your benefit; they help you compare your present spiritual maturity to the biblical principles presented in the lesson. If you're part of a study group, you will not be asked to share any personal answers or information with the group.

A Final Word

Throughout this study, masculine pronouns are often used in the generic sense to avoid awkward sentence construction. When the pronouns _He_, _Him_, and _His_ are used to refer to the Trinity (God the Father, Jesus Christ the Son, and the Holy Spirit), they always refer to the masculine gender.

This Lamplighters Bible study was written after many hours of careful study. It's our prayer that it helps you **grow in the grace and knowledge of our Lord and Savior Jesus Christ. To Him be the glory both now and forever. Amen** (2 Peter 3:18).

About the Author

John Stewart was raised near Winnipeg, Canada. Drafted by the Pittsburgh Penguins (NHL), he played professional hockey for eight years. In 1977, John accepted Jesus Christ alone for eternal life. He graduated from seminary in 1988 and served as a pastor for fifteen years. During this time, he planted two Bible-believing churches and founded Lamplighters International where he now serves as executive director. John continues to write and speak nationally on the subject of making disciples.

Introduction

Many Christians believe Proverbs is the most helpful book in the Bible. Inspired by its practical nature, many believers faithfully read the chapter of Proverbs that corresponds to the day of the month. Proverbs offers sound instruction on a wide variety of subjects such as interpersonal relationships, personal and professional finance, effective communication, mental health, and business and personal ethics.

Simply reading Proverbs will offer no magical cure for God's people. It must be studied carefully to comprehend its meaning and, unearth its rich spiritual truths. Even the book itself warns us, **Like a thorn that goes into the hand of a drunkard is a proverb in the mouth of fools** (Prov. 26:9).

This brief introduction will help you accurately interpret this divinely inspired portion of God's Word.

Background

The Old Testament was originally written in Hebrew and Aramaic and the New Testament written in common (*koine*) Greek. To the Hebrew, the Old Testament Scriptures divide into three sections: the Law, the Writings, and the Prophets. Two of the three sections are mentioned in Luke 16:31 where the Law = Moses, the writer of the Law. Proverbs is found in the Writings section, along with Job, Ecclesiastes, and a few of the Psalms.

In addition to being part of the Writings, Proverbs is categorized within a smaller classification of Scripture known as Wisdom Literature. Wisdom Literature can be identified by its strong emphasis on the practical aspects of life, its frequent use of questions, and its repetitious appeal for man to evaluate his goals and conduct during his earthly existence.

Bible scholars believe that Solomon's Proverbs were taught to young men in Israel during a period of relative peace to help them understand the importance of exercising wisdom in their daily lives. The absence of war, or its imminent threat, often leads to a superficial approach to life, and the instruction of Proverbs was an appeal to young men to choose the path of wisdom.

Author and Date

Proverbs is comprised of eight sections written at various times by several writers (Prov.1:1; 10:1; 25:1; 30:1; 31:1). King Solomon reigned from 971–931 B.C. and King Hezekiah from 729–686 B.C. This has convinced many Bible scholars that the compilation of Proverbs was completed around 700 B.C. (assuming Agur and Lemuel wrote before then).

What Is a Proverb?

The title of the book comes from the opening phrase, "**The proverbs of Solomon**" (Prov. 1:1). The Hebrew word for proverb *mashal* has the root meaning "to be like" or "to represent." Our English word "proverb" comes from two Latin words, *pro* meaning "for" and *verb* meaning "word."

The biblical Proverbs are short wisdom maxims or truisms offering practical instruction consistent with God's moral order of life. Written in a variety of literary forms (see Literary Form below), they instruct God's people in right spiritual, moral, and social conduct and character. The Proverbs should not be interpreted as absolute universal laws or unconditional promises (see Prov. 26:4–5 where two proverbs appear to contradict).

Literary Form

Students of Proverbs benefit from distinguishing the various types of Proverbs found throughout the book. Many commentators believe the first nine chapters of the book are predominantly a father's exhortations to his son, encouraging him to accept wisdom as the most essential possession of life. The actual Proverbs begin in chapter ten where the two-line proverb dominates.

These various forms or types categorize the Proverbs.

a.   **Connecting Proverbs** (synonymous parallelism). In one of the simplest types of proverbs, two similar ideas are expressed in different words linked by the word "and" (for example, Prov. 11:25).
b.   **Contrasting Proverbs** (antithetical parallelism). In this type of proverb the first line is contrasted in the second and the word "but" often sets apart the contrast (for example, Prov. 10:1).
c.   **Completing Proverbs** (synthetic parallelism). In this type of proverb the second line completes or develops the idea of the first line (for example, Prov. 15:30).
d.   **Cultural Proverbs** (parabolic parallelism). This proverb explains its ethical lesson by a resemblance to natural and everyday life (for example, Prov. 27:15).

Theme

The resounding theme of Proverbs is wisdom - God's wisdom. Proverbs tells what wisdom is, where to find wisdom, the price you pay to gain wisdom, the price you pay to reject wisdom, and how a wise person navigates through various life situations. The words "wise" or "wisdom" occur more than 125 times in the book.

God created the world according to His own moral design. Though marred by the fall of man, this world still functions in many ways according to His creative design. Proverbs gives practical instructions on how man can live in harmony with God's plan. Noted Christian author Warren Wiersbe says, "The wise person believes there is a God, that He is the Creator and Ruler of all things, and that He has put within His creation a divine order that, if obeyed, leads ultimately to success." Success is not acquiring material goods and position, but when man is united with God in salvation and accepts his responsibility to glorify His Creator with his life.

So Where Is Jesus Christ?

The Bible is not simply a moral or ethical handbook — something that educates and inspires us to increase our human efforts to fulfill God's plan for our lives. Rightly understood, the Word of God, including Proverbs, leads us to realize that without salvation through Jesus Christ we will consistently fail to live out God's plan for our lives. The apostle Paul told Timothy that the Holy Scriptures (including Proverbs) **make you wise for salvation through faith which is in Christ** Jesus (2 Tim. 3:15).

God's Word gives His plan for wise living. Jesus Christ died on the cross to give salvation so we can comprehend and live according to the Father's plan. The Holy Spirit gives us the power to live out His plan. Jesus Christ is the perfect example of living life according to the wisdom of God. In Jesus Christ **are hidden all the treasures of wisdom and knowledge** (Col. 2:3).

Importance of This Study

The book of Proverbs applies to all ages of history, but it is particularly relevant to our time and society. Peace and prosperity offer many choices and the false assurance that money and power are the keys to happiness. The wisdom of Proverbs warns us against becoming hapless victims of folly's deceit. Instead, we are to be willing recipients of God's wisdom.

Proverbs sets in antithesis the path to destruction and the path to wise and abundant living. Unfortunately, the victims of folly's deceit are no longer faceless names presented antiseptically in the media. They are friends, neighbors, and even those of our own families. Can this tragedy of human destruction be stopped? Wisdom answers affirmatively as she shouts in the streets lifting up her voice in the square (1:20) and calling to all who will listen. The voice we hear in the square is the wisdom of Proverbs.

Study 1a The Beginning of Wisdom

Read — Introduction, Proverbs 1:1–7; other references as given

In this lesson, you'll learn the historical setting of Proverbs and an overview of its content. The answers to the questions in this lesson are found either in the Introduction on pages two and three, or in the Bible verses listed at the end of the questions.

Before you begin this lesson, humble yourself before God, and ask Him to reveal Himself to you through His inspired Word.

1. God's Word is like a flawless diamond. Each time its pages are turned, it reveals another aspect of God's brilliant nature and His matchless plan for your life. If we embrace the truth, God reveals Himself and we are transformed into the image of Jesus Christ. We gain a new measure of freedom (John 8:32), which enables us to bring glory to His name. What are some of the practical topics addressed in the book of Proverbs?

2. Misinterpreting the Bible has caused hundreds of false religions to come into existence. The result has been ruination of countless lives — all in the name of God. Believers should diligently study the Bible to avoid misusing His Word and spreading error. To what does the Bible compare a proverb when it is misused by a fool (Prov. 26:9)?

3. The Bible is God's inspired revelation to equip you with everything you need to live a life that brings honor to Him. The Old Testament (OT) was originally written in Hebrew and Aramaic and the New Testament (NT) was originally written in Greek. List the three major sections or divisions of the Hebrew OT and circle or underline the section in which the book of Proverbs is found?

4. The Bible is not so much *a book* as it is *a collection of books*. According to most Bible scholars, what was the historical setting of Proverbs?

5. a. Who were the four men or groups God used to contribute to the book of Proverbs (Prov. 1:1; 25:1; 30:1; 31:1)?

    b.   Please give the definition of a biblical proverb?

6.   a.   List four characteristics of a biblical proverb.

        1.

        2.

        3.

        4.

    b.   List the four types of two-line proverbs given in the Introduction.

    c.   What theme dominantes the book of Proverbs?

    d.   Who is the only man who lived his entire life according to the wisdom of God?

7.   Each book of the Bible provides an indispensable contribution to the believer's understanding of God. Why is it so important for Christians to study Proverbs?

8. Now that you've gained a better understanding of the background of Proverbs, let's study the book itself. The first six verses tell us several benefits a person can gain from thoroughly studying and applying the wisdom of Proverbs. What are they (Prov.1:2–6)?

9. The Bible says **All Scripture is given by inspiration of God, and is profitable for doctrine** (how to live right), **for reproof** (how to know where you went wrong), **for correction** (how to get back on the right path), **for instruction in righteousness** (how to stay on the right path; 2 Tim. 3:16).

    a. The Word of God will help everyone who humbly and thoroughly studies it. What four groups of people will receive specific instruction from studying Proverbs (Prov.1:4-5)?

    b. What *do you think* is the difference between the simple man and the young man (Prov.1:4)?

10. **A wise man will hear and increase learning**, but **fools despise wisdom and instruction** (Prov. 1:5, 7). What specific things are you doing to gain wisdom and increase your knowledge of God and His ways so that you can bring more glory to His name?

11. What is the first step a person must take to gain real knowledge about living wisely (Prov.1:7)?

Study 1b   The Beginning of Wisdom

Read — Proverbs 1:8–33; other references as given

The people with whom you associate will greatly influence your life. God warns us, **Evil company corrupts good habits** (1 Cor. 15:33). In this lesson we hear two voices calling — the voice of folly (Prov.1:10–19) and the voice of wisdom (Prov. 1:20–33). The voice we listen to leads to the path of life or to the path of destruction.

Before you begin this lesson, humble yourself before God, and ask Him to reveal Himself to you through His inspired Word.

12. Many people are confused over who holds primary responsibility for rearing children within a society. Some think it's the government's responsibility; others think it is the church's responsibility; still others think the children themselves are responsible. (This last philosophy of child rearing is often seen in the "affirmation-parenting model" whereby parents believe their main goal is to affirm their child's decisions and choices. This philosophy is based on the false concept that all truth is relative.)

    a. Who has God given the primary responsibility of instructing children (**son**) in the various aspects of wise and skillful living (Prov.1:8; Deut. 6:4–8; Eph. 6:1–4)?

    b. If you're a parent, how are you faithfully fulfilling this important spiritual responsibility? If you are single, do you think a commitment to assume this God-given responsibility should be a prerequisite to marriage?

13. A portion of the Bible was written in metaphorical language. (A metaphor is a figure of speech in which a word or phrase compares one thing to another, helping the reader understand the original thought more fully.) For example, Jesus compared our receptivity to the Word to four types of soil (Mark 4:3–9). The text in Proverbs 1:9 compares godly parental instruction to a garland, or graceful ornament, on a young person's head and chains around their neck. What do you think this metaphor teaches us?

14. The Hebrew words for **simple** (v. 4) and **entice** (v. 10) come from the same Hebrew root (*pathah*), which means "to be open or spacious." When referring to a person, it means "to be open to any opinion/perspective or uncommitted."

    a. What does this teach us about who is most susceptible to evil's solicitation (Prov. 1:4, 7, 10)?

    b. Give four characteristics of sinners who prey on the uncommitted person (Prov. 1:10–19).

    c. Who is harmed by their sin (Prov. 1:11, 18–19)?

15. a. The primary motive of these fools' attack is financial gain (Prov. 1:13). What are some modern examples of financially motivated attacks on the innocent or unsuspecting?

    b. What arguments do these social and moral rebels use to enlist the help of naive or foolish people (Prov.1:10–14)?

16. It's been said that a smart man learns from his mistakes, a wise man learns from the mistakes of others, but a fool learns from neither. What two reasons did the father give his son to encourage him to resist sin's enticement (Prov.1:10–19)?

17. Wisdom is personified as a woman lifting up her voice in the open square, crying at the head of the noisy streets and at the gates of the city (Prov. 1:20–21).

    a. What do you think this imagery tells us about acquiring wisdom?

b. Take a minute to review the meaning of the Hebrew root for **simple** and **entice** (see question #14). Now restate in your own words the first question in Proverbs 1:22.

c. What specific spiritual commitments have you made to ensure that you and those you love do not become a gullible victim of evil men and women?

18. Refusing wisdom's call causes serious consequences. Please name at least four (Prov.1:24–33).

19. Even knowing there is grave danger in refusing wisdom's call, millions of people reject God and His appeal to help them through life. They may turn to God in times of trouble only to find that wisdom will not answer the fool in the day of his calamity (Prov. 1:24–31).

a. In the New Testament book of James, the writer tells us that God gives wisdom **to all liberally and without reproach** (James 1:5). How can the promise of James and the warning of Proverbs 1:24–31 both be true?

b. Why do so many people reject the wisdom of God (Mark 4:14–19; John 3:19; 1 Cor. 2:14; Heb. 4:2)?

Study 2a   Why Study the Bible?

Read — *Proverbs 2:1–3:35; other references as given*

The grand plans we announce to others are not as important as the daily decisions we make. For it is the daily decisions sometimes—small and apparently insignificant — that often dictate our future.

One life-changing decision many Christians make is taking time daily to study God's Word and pray. But many struggle for years to establish a personal time with God and His Word. In this lesson, you'll discover the essential keys to effective personal Bible study.

Before you begin this lesson, humble yourself before God, and ask Him to reveal Himself to you through His inspired Word.

1. The first nine chapters of Proverbs are a series of sermons, or fatherly talks, to a son and other children. The first use of the phrase **my son** (Prov. 1:8) identifies the beginning of the first sermon or talk. The frequent use of the phrase **my son** (Prov. 3:11, 21; 4:10, 20; 5:1; 6:1, 3, 20; 7:1) makes it clear that the father longs to have his son embrace the path of wisdom.

    a. What do you think are the words and commandments the father refers to in Proverbs 2:1?

    b. Why do you think the father refers to wisdom as **my words** and **my commands** if all wisdom comes from God (Prov. 2:1)?

2. The word **treasure** (Prov. 2:1; KJV — "hide"; NIV — store up") teaches the first essential spiritual truth every Christian must understand before acquiring the wisdom of God. What is this truth?

3. Do you think the words **ear, heart,** and **voice** (Prov. 2:2–3) represent various religious duties (for example, listening, meditating on Scripture, praying) that must be done to acquire wisdom, or is the writer simply saying that man's total being must be fully engaged in this endeavor (Prov. 2:2–4)?

4. a. An important two-word phrase is repeated three times in Proverbs 2:1–4. The repetition of this phrase helps us understand another essential key in gaining the wisdom of God. What is it?

    b. What do you think the repetition of this phrase (**if you**) teaches about acquiring wisdom?

5. In the Western world, silver is not considered as precious a metal as gold. In the Old Testament, however, silver is mentioned before gold (except in Deuteronomy and Chronicles), indicating its superior value to the ancient Israelites. Silver was the standard for business transactions and was weighed out for payment of purchases and wages. Restate Proverbs 2:4 in your own words, substituting two modern words for silver and hidden treasures, or gold.

6. Eight disciplines, or spiritual commitments, must be made before a believer can acquire the knowledge of God (Prov. 2:1–4). The knowledge referred to in this passage is not related to salvation but rather to the practical wisdom that enables a believer to comprehend God's plan for abundant living. In salvation, man is the recipient of God's free gift of eternal life (Rom. 6:23). If you are not sure that you are born again and have received God's free gift of salvation, please turn to "The Final Exam" to learn how you can receive the free gift of salvation. However, to acquire the wisdom of God, a believer must diligently pursue God and His revelation. In what way(s) do you think understanding the difference between how man is saved and how he gains wisdom should affect your Christian life?

7. After listing the prerequisites for gaining the wisdom of God (Prov.2:1–4) the biblical passage changes abruptly beginning in Proverbs 2:5.

    a. In what way(s) does the word **then** (Prov. 2:5, 9) affect the promises of blessing in Proverbs 2:5–12?

b.   Some view the disciplined study of biblical truth as an academic pursuit void of real practical benefit. Name at least seven practical benefits gained from diligently studying God's Word (Prov. 2:5–16).

c.   When we diligently pursue God's Word knowledge becomes pleasant to our souls (Prov. 2:10). What important truths does this passage teach about our initial and continuing relationship to wisdom (Prov. 2:1–10)?

8.   Proverbs 2:6 holds an excellent parallel definition of wisdom. What is it?

9.   If you seek wisdom with all your heart, discretion will preserve and protect you (Prov. 2:11). Discretion includes the ability to evaluate multiple options in life and to choose the best one (Prov. 2:12).

a.   What two groups or individuals will discretion keep us from being trapped by (Prov. 2:11–16)?

b.   One of the ways we can discern between wise men and wicked men is by evaluating their speech (Prov. 2:12, 17). Name two speech patterns of ungodly people that indicate they do not follow the path of uprightness (Prov. 2:12–16).

c.   List some examples of ungodly or perverse speech you've listened to in the past three months.

d.   What personal spiritual decisions have you made to avoid this contamination?

10.   Proverbs 2:16–19 gives a vivid example of one whose ways are crooked and who lives in darkness. Because of her immoral conduct, the strange woman or adulteress (Hebrew *zarah*; the adulteress represents all immoral people, both men and women), is estranged from the corporate life of Israel. With what two persons has she broken covenant (Prov. 2:17)?

Study 2b   Why Study the Bible?

Read — *Proverbs 2:1–3:35; other references as given*

An old American proverb reads, "Sow a thought, reap a habit; sow a habit, reap a lifestyle, sow a lifestyle, reap a destiny." A person who says "I can't help what I think. This is just how I am feeling" fails to realize that his feelings are nothing more than an emotional extension of his thoughts. If we have trouble with "runaway" emotions or feelings, we must allow God to take control of our thoughts, and our feelings will follow. The apostle Paul said, **casting down arguments and every high thing that exalts itself against the knowledge of God, bringing every thought into captivity to the obedience of Christ** (2 Cor. 10:5).

In this lesson, you'll discover the close relationship between right thinking (the wisdom of God) and right living. Before you begin this lesson, humble yourself before God, and ask Him to reveal Himself to you through His inspired Word.

11. In Proverbs 3:1, the godly father continues to appeal to his son to gain wisdom. What do you think the repetition of the phrase **my son** and the constant appeals for him to gain wisdom teach parents about their role in instructing children in the things of God? If you're a child still living under your parents' authority, how does this passage help you understand your parents' role in instructing you?

12. Proverbs 3:1–10 gives five proverbial or general promises (Prov. 3:2, 4, 6, 8, 10). The first, second, and fifth should not be interpreted as unconditional promises (Eccl. 7:15; Isa. 53:2–3; John 1:11; 1 Cor. 4:9–12). Each one is preceded by a human obligation before the anticipated benefit can be realized (vv. 1, 3, 5, 7, 9).

    a. What benefits are we likely to receive if we diligently keep the commandments of God (Prov. 3:1–2)?

    b. What do you think it means to bind around your neck **mercy and truth** (Prov. 3:3; NIV — "love and faithfulness"; the Hebrew *hesed* is very difficult to translate into English, resulting in various translations)?

    c. In what ways do you think these two qualities contribute to favor with God and man?

13. Before the fall of man (Gen. 3:1–6), Adam lived in perfect harmony with God (Gen. 1:31; 2:19, 25). His sole desire was to obey God. During that time, Adam was *perfect* (without defect) — but not *perfected* (confirmed in righteousness). Adam's failure in the Garden moved him away from God and into complicity with Satan. Since the fall, man does not naturally obey God. In fact, in his natural state (before salvation) he hides from God, values his own thoughts and ways above God's, and bears eternal consequences for his estrangement from God.

   a. Sometimes Christians claim God's promises without realizing there may be conditions to meet before the promise is realized. Restate in your own words the three prerequisites (Prov. 3:5–6) that must be met before God's promise of divine guidance can be claimed in Proverbs 3:6.

   b. Do you think the phrases **trust in the Lord with all your heart** and **lean not on your own understanding** are basically synonymous (Prov. 3:5)? If not, what is the distinction between the two?

14. Is there anything in your life (sinful habits, thoughts, or attitudes you know are disobedient to God's Word) that proves you do not trust the Lord with all your heart — things that prevent you from being confident that the Lord is guiding you?

15. Humility and virtuous living (Prov. 3:7-8) bring healing and refreshment to our lives because they are evidence we're living in harmony with God's will (Prov. 4:20–22). God also commands us to **honor the Lord with your possessions and with the first fruits of all your increase** (Prov. 3:9). List two important truths this verse teaches about giving to the Lord's work.

16. Believers should willingly submit to another aspect of spiritual development (Prov. 3:11–12). Name at least four benefits a believer receives when he responds correctly to the discipline of the Lord (Prov. 3:12; Psalm 119:67, 71; Heb. 10:10-12, 12:7–9).

17. Wisdom is more profitable than silver, yields a better return than gold, and is more precious than rubies (Prov. 3:13–15). In fact, no investment you'll ever make can compare to wisdom (Prov. 3:15). What spiritual dividends, or return-on-investment, can you expect to receive if you embrace God's wisdom (Prov. 3:17–18)?

18. If you think wisdom is something new, it's not! It is not a new social or business fad, adopted by the culturally elite as the latest buzzword. Wisdom has been around for ages. What does the writer of Proverbs say about how wisdom was used in the past, which should convince you to adopt it as a lifetime passion and pursuit (Prov. 3:19–20)?

19. Again the writer of Proverbs exhorts the son to not lose sight of wisdom and discretion (Prov. 3:21). What additional benefits does the father say the son will receive if he gains wisdom (Prov. 3:22–26)?

20. The relationship between submitting to God and virtuous living is inescapable. Unfortunately, moral behavior and ethics within the Christian community are almost indistinguishable from the world at large. When this happens, God is dishonored, the testimony of the church of Jesus Christ is marred, and precious opportunities for reaching the lost are wasted. From the following verses, restate the moral requirements God expects from those who claim to be His followers.

   a.   Proverbs 3:27–28

   b.   Proverbs 3:29–30

21. Of the four literary forms of proverbs described in the Introduction, which form is found in Proverbs 3:33–35?

Study 3a   The Principal Thing

Read — Proverbs 4:1–5:23; other references as given

Pursuing wisdom must not be a weekend hobby — a casual thirty-minute Sunday investment in the eternal. Warren Wiersbe says, "Wisdom is not for the curious, but it is for the serious. There is a price to pay if you would gain wisdom, but there is a greater price to pay if you don't. The most expensive thing in the world is sin."

Before you begin this lesson, humble yourself before God, and ask Him to reveal Himself to you through His inspired Word.

1.   The change from son (Prov. 3:1) to children (Prov. 4:1) probably indicates that the teaching (Prov. 4:1–9) is more traditional in nature. Nevertheless, the father's relentless pursuit to help his son(s) gain wisdom continues.

   a.   Survey the father's instruction to his son to this point in the book of Proverbs. What words would you use to describe the father's continuing efforts to help his children adopt the wisdom of God?

   b.   If you are a parent, how would you compare the father's efforts to your present attempts to educate your child(ren) in the wisdom of God?
   If you are a Christian single, do you have a similar passion for the spiritual advancement of others?

   c.   What did the apostle Paul say about his own efforts to see Jesus Christ formed in the lives of others (Gal. 4:19)?

2.   In Proverbs 3:19–20, the writer said God used wisdom in the act of creation. The point is clear: If God employed wisdom to create the world, establish the heavens, and bring about the flood during the days of Noah (**all the fountains of the great deep were broken up**; Gen. 7:11), how much more does man need wisdom.

   a.   In Proverbs 4:3–9 the writer uses another argument to help his children understand the importance of gaining wisdom. What is it?

    b.   What words and phrases did the grandfather use to describe the wisdom of God (Prov. 4:3–9)?

3.   In addition to the words and phrases used in this and other passages of Scripture, God's people use other terms to describe the truth and wisdom of God — divinely inspired, inerrant, etc. On the other hand, non-Christians use terms such as obsolete, outdated, irrelevant, fictional, anecdotal, and mythical to describe God's Word.

    a.   Why do unsaved people (natural man) often describe the Word of God in such negative terms (1 Cor. 2:14)?

    b.   What or who prevents them from understanding the truth of God (2 Cor. 4:4)?

4.   Gaining God's wisdom is not an option to be considered — it is a passion to be pursued. If you put the pursuit of wisdom before all things, God will honor your commitment and bless your life (Prov. 4:6, 8–12).

    a.   What specific commitment(s) do you think you should consider making to gain the wisdom of God?

    b.   Many believers make a spiritual commitment to read and study God's Word every day in order to gain the wisdom of God. Have you ever made this commitment?

5.   Wisdom will guide you into the right paths of life (Prov. 4:11) and keep you from the evil way (Prov. 4:14). The writer of Proverbs instructs us to avoid the paths of the wicked entirely (Prov. 4:14–15). Yet, the apostle Paul said we are to live **in the midst of a crooked and perverse generation, among whom you shine as lights**

in the world (Phil. 2:14). How can a believer avoid the paths of the wicked fulfilling the biblical responsibility to live within a wicked and perverse society (Rom. 12:1–2)?

6. The wicked are so bent on doing evil that a day cannot go by without them planning and executing evil plans (Prov. 4:16). What will they ultimately receive for the diligent execution of their schemes (Prov. 4:17, 19)?

7. While the wicked stumble in the darkness of their own deception, the path of the righteous becomes brighter and brighter (Prov. 4:18). Do you think **the perfect day** (Prov. 4:18; NIV — "the first light of day") refers to the time when we are in heaven (the path of righteousness will become more and more clear until we die), or does the phrase simply refer to the time when the sun has fully risen?
Why?

8. The father repeatedly taught his son and his other children to pursue wisdom. What other things did the father tell his son to do to help him live wisely throughout his life (Prov. 4:20–27)?

9. In three words, summarize the father's instruction to this point (Prov. 1:2–4:27).

Study 3b   The Principal Thing

Read — Proverbs 4:1–5:23; other references as given

    The writer of Proverbs moves from warning his son about associating with ungodly people in general to identifying a specific individual he must avoid at all costs — the immoral woman. (In Study 2a, she was identified as representing immoral men and women of all ages.) The father instructs his son on the characteristics of immoral people and the devastating consequences of being caught in their web of destruction.

    Before you begin this lesson, humble yourself before God, and ask Him to reveal Himself to you through His inspired Word.

10. The **immoral woman** (Hebrew *zarah*, sometimes translated "stranger," "strange woman," or "harlot") was estranged from the Israelite community because of her immoral behavior and her willful violation of the Law of God given to Moses on Mount Sinai. There's a big difference between the type of speech the father wants his son to have and the kind of speech spoken by an immoral woman. What is the difference (Prov. 4:20–22, 24; 5:3–5)?

11. Proverbs chapters 5 through 7 present the most complete profile of an immoral person in the Bible. Describe in your own words the true character of this instrument of human destruction (Prov. 5:4–6, 8–9, 20).

12. The Bible teaches unequivocally that God's people are to be morally pure. Believers should abstain from all forms of sexual activity outside the bonds of marriage. What does the apostle Paul tell the Thessalonians about sexual purity (1 Thess. 4:3–8)?

13. In recent years, public school systems throughout the nation have rigorously debated the subject of sex education, including homosexuality. Throughout church history, homosexuality has been considered sinful and the church was undivided in its position against it. In 1948, Dr. Alfred Kinsey released his famous study on sexuality, stating that 10 percent of the American male population was homosexual. (He released a similar study on women's sexuality in 1953.) Even though Dr. Judith

Reisman has exposed Dr. Kinsey's work as fraudulent (_Kinsey: Crimes and Consequences_), anti-sodomy laws have been overturned and tens of thousands of school-aged children are now taught that homosexuality is an acceptable lifestyle.

a. What does the Bible teach about homosexuality (Rom. 1:26–28; 1 Cor. 6:9–11)?

b. What do you think individual believers can do to help the public understand the truth about homosexuality and to protect the nation's children against the pro-homosexual indoctrination they face in public schools?

14. a. What will the person lacking moral discretion receive for his or her indulgence (Prov. 5:4–5, 10–14)?

b. Proverbs 5:11 warns that immorality can destroy our flesh. Please give some examples of this truth in our society.

15. a. Name three individuals whose lives and witness for God were marred by immoral behavior (Gen. 49:3–4; 2 Sam. 11:1–4; 13:10–15).

b. The father gives two important pieces of advice to his son regarding association with the immoral woman (Prov. 5:8; 6:25). What are they?

16. An important principle about moral purity is repeated in the Song of Solomon (Song of Solomon 2:7; 3:5; 5:8; 8:4). This moral principle will help believers of all ages avoid sexual immorality. Restate this important biblical truth in your own words.

17. In many parts of the world, access to drinkable water is a matter of life or death. Sometimes, pollutants contaminated ancient public water sources.

    a.   What or whom do you think is represented by the cistern (Prov. 5:15)?

    b.   What important truth(s) about moral behavior do you think is illustrated by this figure of speech (the cistern; Prov. 5:15)?

18. The immoral person acquires bitterness of soul, disgrace, and perhaps even physical affliction from violating God's moral law (Prov. 5:4, 11; 6:33). What words are used to describe the person who commits himself to moral purity within the marriage bond (Prov. 5:18–19)?

19. The young man is encouraged to be enraptured with the wife of his youth rather than with a strange woman (Prov. 5:19–20). The Hebrew word (*sagah*) can mean **intoxicated** or a **staggering gait**. In this context, it refers to the sexual infatuation an individual should have for his or her marriage partner. What important truths do these two verses teach us about marriage (Prov. 5:18–19)?

20. Why should Christians abstain from all forms of immorality (Prov. 5:21–23)?

Study 4a   How to Avoid Entrapment

Read — *Proverbs 6:1–7:27; other references as given*

In the previous chapter, the father warned his son about becoming entrapped by an immoral woman. Now he warns him against other forms of entrapment: financial entrapment (Prov. 6:1–5), personal sin, including indolence (Prov. 6:6–11, 16–19), slick schemers (Prov. 6:12–15), and having a sexual affair with a married person (Prov. 6:20–35).

Before you begin this lesson, humble yourself before God, and ask Him to reveal Himself to you through His inspired Word.

1.   The father warns his son about placing too much confidence in the shallow promises of future financial gain made by strangers (Prov. 6:1–5; Hebrew *reᵃ ...zar* — "neighbor, stranger"). Immature and misguided faith that focuses solely on the words of others often leads to financial entrapment and hinders the person's future usefulness for God.

     a.   What advice did the father give his son if he found himself entrapped by a foolish financial pledge (Prov. 6:1–5)?

     b.   The father used two vivid word pictures to help his son see the need and manner by which he should escape from this trap. What do you think pictures of the gazelle and bird taught the son (Prov. 6:5)?

2.   When a society becomes litigious (dominated by lawsuits and other legal actions), there is often a dangerous shift from what is right and wrong to what is legal and illegal. If Christians fall prey to this moral dilemma, they may rationalize sin and focus more on the legal code than on God's Word. What does God say about the words we speak and our responsibility to others for them (Prov. 6:1–5; Matt. 5:33–37)?

3.   How can a believer keep himself from becoming entrapped by personal commitments about the future when things may change (James 4:13–17)?

4. It's likely the father intended to warn his son against the individual promising quick financial gain in exchange for a loan. The Hebrew word (*re*ᵃ *...zar*) for stranger (Prov. 6:1; NIV — "another") is a person whose only affiliation to the son is the promise of mutual financial benefit. The father directs his son's attention to one of God's unique creatures, the ant, as an example of diligent labor that is rewarded (Prov. 6:6–11). List two things all lazy and indolent people can learn from the ant (Prov. 6:6–8). If you're a parent of young children, perhaps together you can observe an anthill to teach a proper work ethic.

5. Many Christians have a misguided concept of work. Rather than working hard and being a good witness for Christ to their employer, some Christians think work is a curse. Yet, they believe God will somehow bless their indolence. What does the Bible say about a sluggard (Prov. 6:9–11)?

6. Wicked people often try to take advantage of others. They routinely use deceptive body language to "cover their tracks," trying to avoid being trapped by their words in the future when their deceit is exposed.

    a. What kinds of sinister sign language do these scoundrels often use to deceive others (Prov. 6:12–14)?

    b. God is watching them as they scheme to deceive others. What will they receive in the end for their wickedness (Prov. 6:15)?

7. God hates not only the works of darkness but also the attitudes from which they are generated (Prov. 6:16–19). The phrase (**six things the Lord hates, yes seven**; Prov. 6:16) is a Hebrew figure of speech known as a numerical ladder. It's used to show that the present list is not exhaustive. In other words, there are other things that the Lord hates and that are an abomination to Him (Lev. 18:22; Deut. 23:18; Prov. 8:7; 11:1).

    a. List the seven things that God hates and are abominations to Him (Prov. 6:16–19)?

b. Of these seven things God hates, in which ones have you engaged in the past three months?
    God promises full forgiveness to those who come to Him in sincere repentance. If you committed any of these sins, ask God to forgive you and cleanse you (1 John 1:9). If you're not sure you are a child of God, please read "The Final Exam" in the back of this manual carefully. It will help you understand how you can become a born again Christian.

8. In Proverbs 6:20–35, the father returns to a familiar source of entrapment — the immoral woman. This time the immoral woman is further identified as an adulteress (a married woman; Prov. 6:26, 32, 34–35). The son is encouraged to heed the instruction of both the father and the mother so he can be on guard at all times **(When you roam, when you sleep, when you awake**; Prov. 6:20–22). What words are used to describe the woman who violates the marriage covenant she made before God to her husband (Prov. 6:24–26)?

9. Many celebrities (movie stars, music stars, pro athletes) flaunt their immoral behavior on television and radio talk shows. They talk about "starter marriages," "significant others" (a live-in lover), and "serial divorce" as if nothing is wrong. Consequently, many Christians have become confused, adopting a shallow, non-biblical view of morality. When a society becomes morally confused, God's people must realize His Word is true and His standard for morality does not change, regardless of the apparent lack of observable consequences.

    a. What does the Bible teach in the following verse about His standard for moral behavior (1 Cor. 6:18–20; Heb. 13:4)?

    b. What will the individual (Christian or non-Christian) receive for his folly if he violates God's moral standard by becoming sexually involved with a married woman (Prov. 6:26–29, 31–35)?

Study 4b   How to Avoid Entrapment

Read — Proverbs 6:1–7:27; other references as given

Before you begin this lesson, humble yourself before God, and ask Him to reveal Himself to you through His inspired Word.

10. Again the believer is encouraged to gain the wisdom of God before facing the trials of life. Theologian Larry Pettegrew said, "Don't throw away truth just because you don't think you need it today. It is like money in the bank. You will need it sooner or later." What words or phrases are used to describe the level of intimacy God's people ought to have with wisdom before they actually employ it in real-life situations (Prov. 7:1–4)?

11. In his relentless appeal to his son to gain wisdom, the father isn't promoting some spiritual exercise to occupy his son's time, filling the listless hours of early adolescence. Wisdom offers intensely practical benefits to those who embrace it. Countless lives of intelligent men and women have been destroyed by a lapse in moral conduct. Among the fallen are kings, high-ranking politicians (including presidents), business and civic leaders, church leaders, and many others.

    a. In Proverbs 7:6–27, the father graphically illustrates how an immoral person can trap his son. List the four individuals or groups mentioned in this illustration (Prov. 7:6–10)?

    b. If you were asked to present a modern circumstance or setting where sexual entrapment of a similar nature might take place, what picture comes to mind?

12. a. List three things about the young man's thinking and conduct that make him an easy target for the immoral woman (Prov. 7:7–9)?

b. Name at least five characteristics of the immoral woman that will help you identify such a person and protect you from being trapped by this sort of individual (Prov. 6:24–25; 7:10–15; 9:13–18).

13. Gone are the days when a man had to visit the "red light" district of a city, risking arrest by some undercover vice squad. (Many cities post the names of the "Johns" in their local newspapers, a fulfillment of Proverbs 6:33.) Gone also are the days when a man had to frequent a seedy adult bookstore to purchase a sleazy pornographic magazine or video. The Internet now allows men and women to enter the dark world of immoral behavior within their own homes and workplaces. Adult pornographic websites receive hundreds of thousands of hits every day by people at work and at home — all with the same result: broken lives, shattered innocence, guilt, and destroyed families.

    a. Have you looked at pornography in any form (Internet, videos, magazines) in the past year?

    b. What recommendation would you give someone who confided in you that they have a problem with pornography?

14. The seductress is dressed like a harlot, and she aggressively seeks her prey (Prov. 7:10, 13). As part of her crafty seduction, she tells the young man she has paid her peace offerings (Prov. 7:14). These fellowship offerings refer to the meat left over from the votive offering she made at the sanctuary (Lev. 7:11–21). It appears she was informing the young man that she had meat for him to eat and that she was ceremonially clean, perhaps after her menstrual cycle.

    a. She boldly propositions the young man with promises of a night of unbridled love (Prov. 7:16–18). Like many, she appears to be confused about the difference between love and lust. What is the difference (2 Sam. 13:1–15; 1 Cor. 13:4–7)?

b. First Corinthians 13:4–7 gives fifteen qualities of genuine biblical love. Of the fifteen, eight are presented in the negative. In other words, true love restricts its behavior for the benefit of others and for the glory of God. Which of the eight restrictive qualities of love do you need to ask God to help you develop more fully?

15. The adulteress' final words of enticement assure the young man they will not be caught because her husband was away for a long time (Prov. 7:19–20). With persuasive speech (literally, "the greatness of her words"), she causes him to yield. He goes, not knowing that he follows her as **an ox goes to the slaughter** (Prov. 7:22). What additional words and phrases are used to help the young man understand the destruction that lies ahead (Prov. 7:22–27)?

16. The solicitation of young men (and women) to engage in immoral behavior is not isolated to clandestine meetings between consenting adults in darkened alleys. An endless river of moral sewage from television, movies, videos, books, magazines, and the Internet flows into the average young person's life. Sex education programs in public school encourage students to "wait until they are ready," rather than promoting God's standard of (sexual) abstinence until marriage. Some public schools even provide pro-homosexual counseling resources to students who question their sexual identity. How do you think individual Christians, including you, and churches can do a better job of protecting America's youth in this area?

Study 5a   The Excellence of Wisdom

Read — *Proverbs 8:1–9:18; other references as given*

Proverbs chapters 8 and 9 are Solomon's final appeal to his son to gain wisdom. Then, he begins presenting two-line proverbs (Proverbs 10:1). The two-line proverbs remain obscure riddles if we fail to make wisdom our primary pursuit.

Before you begin this lesson, humble yourself before God, and ask Him to reveal Himself to you through His inspired Word.

1. Throughout the first nine chapters of Proverbs, wisdom and folly are personified and contrasted by two women — folly and wisdom. Folly is a crafty seductress who promises pleasure but delivers pain. She is secretive, devious, and manipulative, and those who follow her ways eventually become the wounded and the slain of this world. She works in the darkness and preys on the simple and naive.

    a. To whom does wisdom call, and where is her voice heard (Prov. 8:1–5)?

    b. It's often difficult for Christians to know exactly where to find wisdom. Some teachers say to let your conscience be your guide. Others say to let your heart guide you (subjective experience). Still others say to find an "anointed" spiritual leader and follow him. Where should a Christian always look to find God's wisdom (John 17:17)?

    c. How can a Christian continue to gain more wisdom (John 14:21; James 1:5–6)?

2. Wisdom calls to all men, but she makes a special appeal to the simple (to gain prudence) and to fools (to gain understanding; Prov. 8:5). Wisdom attempts to motivate these spiritual deadbeats by declaring she has worthy things to offer them. What words or phrases describe the things wisdom will give you if you seek her with all your heart (Prov. 8:6–11)?

3. The words of wisdom (God's truths and principles) are easy to understand for those who embrace them (**They are all plain to him who understands, and right to those who find knowledge**; Prov. 8:9). It's not a matter of understanding that prevents people from accepting the truth — it is a matter of the will. Author Mark Twain said, "It is not what I don't understand about the Bible that bothers me, it is what I do understand that bothers me." If wisdom is found through knowing and obeying God's Word, what commitments do you think a believer should make to God about submission to the Word of God?

4. The value of wisdom is not just for the simple and naive — it's also for those in positions of power (Prov. 8:5, 16). Wisdom resides with prudence (Hebrew *ormah*), which means wisdom provides the individual who possesses it right knowledge for special circumstances. For example, those in positions of power need wisdom to provide good counsel to others and to avoid the temptation to become prideful of their position and achievements. In addition to those mentioned in Proverbs 8:15–16, in what areas do you think all leaders (fathers, mothers, employers, pastors) need to exercise wisdom?

5. To many people, wisdom seems elusive. They live by God's wisdom in many areas of their lives, but then they rely on their own understanding in some critical area and eventually reap the devastating consequences of their folly. When this happens repeatedly, they become discouraged and give up pursuing wisdom.

    a. What does God promise those who love and diligently seek God and His wisdom (Prov. 8:17; James 1:5)?

    b. What else does God promise those who diligently seek wisdom (Prov. 8:18–21)?

6. In Proverbs 8:22–31, wisdom is pictured as the master craftsman who assisted God during creation. When God finished creating this world, He said it was very good (Gen. 1:31). People talk about Mother Nature or Mother Earth, which robs God of the glory due His name in creation. Many schools and communities also celebrate Earth Day but forget that God is the One who created the earth. On the other hand, many

people, including some Christians, abuse God's creation by treating it like their personal garbage dump. What perspective do you think a Christian should have toward the earth (Gen. 1:28; Psalm 24:1)?

7. The father makes one final appeal to his children to embrace the wisdom of God (Prov. 8:32–9:18). Perhaps the son and other children were saying, "Father, we get the point. You want us to get wisdom. We heard you the first time." Wisdom is much more than knowledge. Someone said, "Wisdom goes beyond mere knowledge. It has an action component to it. Wisdom is God-given knowledge humbly put to work."

   a. In the parable of the wise and foolish builders, the man who built his life on the sand and the man who built his life on the rock were compared to two different individuals. What did the two builders represent (Matt. 7:24–27)?

   b. When was the folly of the man who built his life on the sand revealed (Matt. 7:24–27)?

8. The believers to whom the book of Hebrews was written were encouraged to not follow the example of their ancestors who were delivered from Egypt. During the Exodus, the Israelites were given the Law of God and the promise of entering a land flowing with milk and honey. Why did the ancient Israelites perish in the wilderness even though they had been given the Law of God and His promises (Heb. 4:1–2)?

9. Take a close look at your life before God. In which area(s) of your life are you unwilling to yield completely to God?

   a. Sexual purity (actions, thoughts)

   b. Worship (corporate, private)

   c. Financial stewardship (tithing, helping those in need)

   d. Priorities (God, family, work, leisure)

   e. Forgiveness (unforgiveness, anger, resentment, slander)

Study 5b   The Excellence of Wisdom

Read — Proverbs 8:1–9:18; other references as given

Before you begin this lesson, humble yourself before God, and ask Him to reveal Himself to you through His inspired Word.

10. In the previous chapter, wisdom was pictured as a wise master builder who worked with God to create the world. Now wisdom constructs her own home, prepares a lavish feast, and sends her maidens out to invite the guests (Prov. 9:2–3).

    a.   Who does she invite to her feast (Prov. 9:3–4)?

    b.   What does wisdom offer to serve her guests (Prov. 9:5)? (The obvious answer is bread and wine according to the metaphor, but try to give a more complete answer from the passage.)

11. One of wisdom's invited guests, the scoffer, is unlikely to respond to her invitation (Prov. 9:7–8). (You'll learn more about the characteristics of the scoffer in Lamplighters Proverbs 10–31 Bible Study.) The main body of two-line proverbs begins in the next chapter and a great deal of understanding can be gained if you learn to identify the various types of proverbs.

    a.   Proverbs 9:7 gives an excellent example of one of the four types of proverbs. Which type of proverb is found in this verse (see the Introduction, page three, for the various types of proverbs)?

    b.   If you study the parallelism of the proverb found in Proverbs 9:7, you'll better understand the verse. Opposite the word or phrase listed below, give the word or phrase the writer used.

        1.   Correct _____

        2.   Scoffer (NIV — "mocker") _____

        3.   Gets shame (NIV — "invites insult") _____

12. Why do you think unsaved people (those who are not born again according to the Bible) do not accept God and His wisdom, when they offer so many great benefits (John 3:19–20; 2 Cor. 4:4)?

13. It seems natural that those who've never been born again would reject the truth. The Bible, however, teaches that many of God's people have never learned to wholeheartedly embrace truth.

    a. What explanation did the apostle Paul give Timothy as to why those professing to be Christians reject the truth (2 Tim. 4:3–4)?

    b. What was Timothy, who was serving as a pastor at the time, to do about this rejection of God and His truth by these professing believers (2 Tim. 4:2, 5)?

14. In light of what you've learned in this Bible Study, take a moment to examine your relationship with God. Do you have a hunger for God and His Word consistent with the scriptural prerequisites for gaining wisdom, or do you have "itching ears" that want to hear only those things that please you?

15. What do you think you can do to gain a greater appetite for God and His Word?

16. The first thing a Christian must do to acquire the wisdom of God is understand **the fear of the Lord**, which is **the beginning of wisdom** (Prov. 9:10). Although the phrase **the fear of the Lord** appears frequently in Scripture, many believers do not know what it means. Even the prophet Jonah appeared to be confused during the time he was running from God when he said he **feared the Lord** (Jonah 1:4–9).

a.   If you're going to gain wisdom, you must gain a thorough understanding of the meaning of this phrase. The following verses have been carefully chosen to help you develop an accurate definition of this important phrase (Deut. 10:12; Job 28:28; Psalm 33:8; Prov. 14:26). Write down a key thought or phrase from each verse (on a separate paper) and then write a clear definition of the **fear of the Lord** in your own words.

b.   Most people are afraid of one or more things (failure, physical pain, disease, rejection, poverty, success, death, being alone). Unless these fears are yielded to God, they will control you and keep you from loving and serving God. What is your greatest fear, and how does Satan use it to keep you from trusting and obeying the Lord?

c.   The Bible says that God has not given us a spirit of fear (2 Tim. 1:7). Where, then, do you think fear (except the fear of the Lord) comes from, and what is its cure (Isa. 41:10, 13; 43:1)?

17.   As you conclude this study of Proverbs 1–9, take a minute to reflect on what you've studied. What are the most important spiritual truths you've learned in the first nine chapters of Proverbs?

Study 1a   The Beginning of Wisdom

1.   Interpersonal relations, personal and business finance and ethics, effective communication, mental health.

2.   A thorn in the hand of a drunkard.

3.   The Law, the Prophets, and the Writings.

4.   Solomon was king of Israel during a time of relative peace and prosperity. Bible scholars believe the proverbs of Solomon were taught to the young men of Israel to help them understand the importance of exercising wisdom in daily living. The absence of war, or of its imminent threat, often leads men to adopt a superficial approach to life. The instruction of Proverbs was an appeal to young men to choose the path of wisdom.

5.   a.   Solomon, Lemuel, and Agur.
      b.   A proverb is a short wisdom maxim or truism offering practical instruction consistent with God's moral order of life.

6.   a.   1. They are short and practical. 2. They are presented in a variety of literary forms. 3. They teach right conduct in the moral, spiritual, and social realms of life. 4. They should not be understood as universal promises or laws.
      b.   1.   Connecting Proverbs. Example: There is one who scatters, yet increases more; there is one who withholds more than is right, but it leads to poverty (Prov. 11:24).
            2.   Contrasting Proverbs. Example: A wise son makes a glad father, *but* a foolish son is the grief of his mother (Prov. 10:1).
            3.   Completing Proverbs. Example: The light of the eyes rejoices the heart, and a good report makes the bones healthy (Prov. 15:30).
            4.   Cultural Proverbs. Example: A continual dripping on a very rainy day and a contentious woman are alike (Prov. 27:15).
      c.   The central theme of the book of Proverbs is God's wisdom in daily living — skill in living. Proverbs tells what wisdom is, where to find wisdom, the price you pay to gain wisdom, the price you pay to reject wisdom, and how a wise person navigates through various life situations. The words "wise" or "wisdom" occur more than 125 times in the book.
      d.   Jesus Christ.

7.   Proverbs helps us understand that God has a specific plan for every aspect of our daily lives. He wants us to live skillfully in this world and to conduct our lives in a way that brings His blessing to us and to those around us — one that brings maximum glory to His glorious name.

8.   1.   Proverbs will help us understand wisdom and gain instruction about God and His ways (v. 2).
     2.   Proverbs will help us discern the difference between the sayings of understanding and of folly (v. 2).
     3.   Proverbs will give instruction in wise behavior, righteous living, justice, and equity (v. 3).
     4.   Proverbs will give prudence to those who are naive so they can make wise choices in life (v. 4).
     5.   Proverbs will give knowledge about life and discretion to the young (v. 4).
     6.   Proverbs will help us understand biblical proverbs and figures of speech, the sayings of the wise, and their riddles (v. 6; perhaps parables and other metaphors).

9.   a.   The simple (v. 4), the young (v. 4), and the wise man (v. 5).
     b.   The simple or naive person is open to any and every thought and danger because he is uncommitted to a biblical perspective of life. The youth has not learned to recognize the dangers of life, and his inexperience makes him vulnerable as well.

10. Answers will vary.
11. He must gain a proper fear of the Lord. This means he must acknowledge the authority of God over every aspect of his life. This begins with being born again (see "The Final Exam" in the back of this manual for a clear presentation of God's plan of salvation) and continues throughout life as the individual submits to the authority of God.

Study 1b   The Beginning of Wisdom

12. a.   Both parents are responsible for helping their children develop daily living skills (v. 8; Deut. 6:4–9). It appears, however, that the father is ultimately responsible because of his God-ordained leadership role in the family (Eph. 6:1–4).
     b.   Parent portion of the question — Answers will vary but may include the following: Modeling a godly life before children, consistent times of Bible instruction, active participation of the family in a Bible-believing church, spontaneous discussions applying biblical truth to various aspects of daily living. Unmarried portion of the question — Yes. Accepting this important

responsibility to provide biblical instruction for children should be a major consideration before marriage.

13. A graceful wreath or an ornament provides beauty and enhances appearance. A son or daughter's life is beautified when he or she accepts wise parental instruction. The child's demeanor is often pleasant, and his or her life is attractive beyond physical attributes.

14. a. The solicitation to ungodly adventures is often directed toward those who are dangerously open-minded or naive (the simple). These naive fools often do and say things that let shrewd sinners know they can be taken advantage of. These naive fools associate with wrong people and have no regard for God and His ways.
    b. 1. They are violent (vv. 11, 16). 2. They are aggressively solicitous (vv. 10, 11, 14). 3. They have no respect for the property of others (v. 13). 4. They are self-deceived, oblivious to their own destruction (vv. 18–19). 5. They are greedy (vv. 12–13).
    c. The innocent (v. 11) and themselves (v. 18).

15. a. Answers will vary but could include the following: abortion, child pornography, drug-related crimes, income tax evasion, credit card fraud, insurance fraud, schemes of some tele-evangelists. Other answers can apply.
    b. 1. The simple are offered the opportunity to be accepted into a group (vv. 11, 14). 2. The simple are enticed by the opportunity for easy financial gain, especially when unaware of the risks (v. 13).

16. 1. The father said not to go (v. 10). 2. Innocent people will be hurt, and someone may even die (vv. 11, 15). 3. The scheme these sinners propose is illegal (theft; v. 13). 4. The actions of these moral rebels are sinful and evil (v. 16). Those who participate in these evil deeds will eventually be caught, and their lives will be ruined (vv. 17–19).

17. a. Wisdom is readily available to anyone who takes the time and makes the effort to acquire it.
    b. "How long will you who are uncommitted to God's ways and dangerously open-minded continue to live by your own faulty human reason?" Other answers can apply.
    c. Answers will vary.

18. 1. God will not help them in their time of distress (vv. 24–26). 2. God will not answer prayers in the time of calamity, even if they seek Him diligently (v. 28). 3. God will allow them to reap the full extent of what they've sown (v. 31; this means they'll be given no mercy by God). 4. They will eventually be destroyed by their lack of wisdom

(v. 32). 5. They continue to forfeit God's peace available to all who seek His wisdom (v. 33).

19. a. God's generous offer of wisdom is available to all who make the diligent pursuit of His wisdom a lifetime goal. This promise of James 1:5 does not apply if those who call upon God in the day of their calamity have not diligently sought wisdom before that time. The "but" (James 1:6) says the prayer for wisdom must be asked in faith.

    b. They allow Satan to steal the truth from their minds (Mark 4:15). They allow problems and the trials of life to distract them from pursuing the truth (Mark 4:16–17). They're more concerned about gaining material things than pursuing God (Mark 4:19). They don't want their sins to be exposed (John 3:19). They cannot understand the truth because they're not true Christians (1 Cor. 2:14). They're unwilling to live by faith (Heb. 4:2).

Study 2a   Why Study the Bible?

1. a. In the immediate context, it includes the fatherly admonitions contained in Proverbs 1–9. In the broader context, it includes the actual proverbs (Prov. 10:1) and all the godly instruction the father gives his son throughout his lifetime.

    b. The father referred to the words and commandments of God as *his* words and commandments because he had embraced the wisdom of God for himself. When an individual accepts the wisdom of God by faith, truth becomes his intimate friend and ally. It becomes *his* in the sense that it becomes part of his thinking, his actions, and his character — they are his words and commandments.

2. The individual must understand that most teaching cannot be used immediately. (Wisdom is a treasure to be stored until needed.) Generally, some time will pass before an opportunity occurs whereby the wise instruction will be of great benefit. In the interim, wise instruction helps develop beliefs that produce attitudes and actions that direct the course of the person's life.

3. Man's ears (listening to God's Word), heart (our hearts and wills must be open to God), and voice (praise, singing, speaking God's Word to Him and others) must be fully engaged if he is going to acquire wisdom. However, these three aspects of man's nature are likely used representatively to teach that every aspect of man's being must be passionately engaged if he is going to acquire God's wisdom.

4. a. "If you..." This phrase introduces a series of contingencies or qualifying conditions that must be met before an individual can realize the benefits listed in Proverbs 2:5. These conditions indicate that at least some Christians may be unwilling to exert the spiritual energy necessary to accomplish the task and reap the benefits.

    b. The repetition of the phrase "if you" highlights the importance and significance of the decisions each individual must make if he expects to gain God's wisdom. All conditions must be met before the individual can possess the wisdom of God.

5. Answers will vary.

6. Most Christians need to be more diligent in pursuing God and His wisdom. This doesn't mean they try to live the Christian life in their own power (Gal. 3:1–5). They need to make definite spiritual commitments to pursue God so that He reveals additional truth to them. When they know the truth, they will be set free from the corruption in this world and be able to glorify God with their lives. Too many believers are "waiting on God" when God has clearly instructed them to pursue Him.

7. a. The word "then" makes conditional the promises for wisdom, discernment, and protection from error. All the conditions in Proverbs 2:1–4 must be met before the benefits of Proverbs 2:5 can be claimed.

    b. Believers are promised the following: 1. Understanding the fear of the Lord (v. 5). 2. Knowledge of God's plan for man on earth (v. 5). 3. Wisdom (vv. 6, 10). 4. Divine protection (vv. 7–8). 5. A love for God's truth (v. 10) and discretion (v. 11). 6. Deliverance from evil people (v. 16).

    c. Man's first response to God's Word may not necessarily be thrilling. We must pursue God and His Word by faith, knowing that God honors our efforts and that eventually the truth will become pleasant to our souls.

8. Knowledge and understanding. Knowledge is comprehending God's truth for daily living. Understanding is the wisdom to apply God's principles for daily living in a consistently prudent manner.

9. a. Wicked men (Prov. 2:12–15, "those who leave the paths of uprightness") and immoral women (v. 16).

    b. Ungodly people often speak perverse things — both words and ideas that are contrary to God (v. 12), and they often rejoice over doing evil (v. 14). Immoral people often use flattery and seductive speech to accomplish their sexual objectives (v. 16).

    c. Answers will vary.

    d. Answers will vary.

10. Her husband and God (v. 17). The covenant she made with her husband was before God, even though nothing is mentioned about her relationship with God, other than she is immoral.

Study 2b   Why Study the Bible?

11. Parents should never be discouraged by having to repeat instructions to their children. The fallen nature of man, along with a child's immature mental abilities, makes repeating instructions necessary. Children should realize it's their parents' responsibility to instruct them until truths are firmly ingrained in their lives. When parents repeat truths to their children, it's because the parents think the child has not fully grasped the truth.

12. a. A good, long life filled with peace (v. 2).
    b. A believer should develop an intimate relationship with both mercy and truth, allowing them to be his constant companions. A believer should not lose sight of them as he goes about the affairs of life.
    c. If we're not truthful with God, we forfeit fellowship with Him that results in unanswered prayer, loss of peace, and other negative things. If we're not honest with men, they will discover our deceit and distrust us. If we're not merciful toward others, they naturally pull back from us as a protective measure, which hinders our ability to minister to them.

13. a. 1) A believer must trust the Lord fully. 2) A believer must never rely on his own reason when his thoughts are contrary to God and His Word. 3) A believer must acknowledge God's authority over every aspect of his life.
    b. They are two sides on the same coin. If we trust God with all our hearts, we're not leaning on our own understanding. The first phrase looks at the believer's responsibility toward God, and the second looks at the believer's responsibility toward himself. He is to trust God, not himself. Someone said, "Faith is letting God have the last word when our mind is arguing with His Word."

14. Answers will vary.

15. 1. God is honored when His people give back to Him. 2. God expects His people to give back the first portion of their possessions.

16. 1. We're reassured of His love (Prov. 3:12). 2. We learn to obey the Word of God (Psalm 119:67, 71). 3. We're reminded we are God's children (Heb. 12:7–9). 4. We become more godly or righteous in our daily living (Heb. 10:10–12).

17. The believer gains peace and the tree of life, which symbolizes vitality and fullness of life. The believer's life will also be blessed.

18. The Lord used wisdom to create the earth and heavens. These verses show wisdom was used from the foundation of this cosmos, and those who surrender to God's wisdom place themselves in harmony with the eternal plan of God, including creation.

19. 1. The son will have a beauty to his life and live in safety (vv. 22–23). 2. The son will not stumble through life (v. 23). 3. The son will not live in fear or worry about trouble or sudden tragedy (vv. 24–25). 4. The son will sleep well (v. 24). 5. The son will be confident that the Lord will be his guide (v. 26).

20. a. Christians should give according to their means and repay others without delay. They should not offer feeble excuses (lies) to avoid financial and other social debts.
    b. Christians should never devise evil against their neighbors. Perhaps the reference here is to groundless lawsuits against acquaintances and others. Another possibility could be phony legal actions against insurance companies for the sake of gaining a claim, which will be paid by the policyholders, including some of the person's neighbors.

21. They are both Contrasting Proverbs.

Study 3a   The Principal Thing

1. a. Answers will vary. The answer should include words such as relentless, passionate, convicted, diligent, determined, committed, faithful, or responsible. Other answers can apply.
   b. Answers will vary. Answers will vary.
   c. Paul said he agonized like a woman in labor over the Galatian believers' spiritual development. The Greek word *morphow* ("form") means the essential form rather than mere outward shape. Paul was saying he was willing to experience labor-like contraction pains until Christ-like character was formed in the Galatian believers.

2. a. The wisdom the father desired to pass to his son had been passed from a previous generation. The son's grandfather taught principles of wisdom to the son's father when he was young.

The point is this: Wisdom is not new. It's been family treasure for generations. Perhaps the special bond that often exists between grandparents and grandchildren had a special appeal to the son.

b. My words and my command (v. 4), understanding, words of my mouth (v. 5), love her (v. 6), the principal thing (v. 7), exalt and honor (v. 8), ornament of grace and crown of glory (v. 9).

3. a. Unsaved people have no spiritual capacity to comprehend the things of God apart from the enlightening ministry of the Holy Spirit. Because he cannot understand, they're foolishness to him, and he often ridicules them and the people who talk about them. At the time of salvation, the natural man is born again and receives the Spirit of God, which enables him to begin comprehending God and His Word. (For a complete explanation about how to be born again according to the Bible, please read "The Final Exam" in the back of this manual.)

b. The god of this world, or Satan, blinds the minds of all people in the world. This prevents them from understanding truth. Only salvation through Jesus Christ can remove this spiritual blindness and reveal the truth to them.

4. a. Answers will vary.

b. Answers will vary.

5. A believer must present himself to God as a living sacrifice. This means he must "take his stand with Jesus" and turn his back on the world's acceptance and its lusts. A believer must actively resist every attempt of Satan and the corrupt world to force him to adopt its values, goals, and priorities. He should never allow himself to be conformed to this world. He must allow his mind to be renewed and transformed into the image of Jesus Christ. At the very least, he should submit himself to the regular preaching of God's Word and engage in personal Bible study. He should seek to live a godly life within an ungodly world, where he is to shine as light in the darkness and bring others to a saving knowledge of Jesus Christ. (Monasticism has appealed to believers throughout the history of the church, but it has generally failed. God wants us to be "salt and light" by living holy lives. When believers separate from a society, they remove themselves from the people Jesus died for and wants to rescue from eternal judgment.)

6. They reap what they have sown — wickedness and violence (v. 17). They also experience confusion because of forsaking God's offer of wisdom and its promise of divine guidance (v. 19). The law of "sowing and reaping" has three principles every believer would be wise to remember: 1) We always reap the same thing we sow. 2) We always reap sometime later than we sow. 3) We usually reap more than we sow.

7. The time when the sun has fully risen. The second possible interpretation is an example of "allegorical interpretation," or it is sometimes called spiritualizing a verse. This happens when the student assigns an incorrect "hidden" spiritual meaning to a verse. The verse should be understood at face value unless it is obviously a metaphor. Allegorical interpretation often leads to an incorrect interpretation of Scripture.

8. The father told his son to make wisdom the focus of his life (v. 21). He told his son to keep or guard his heart (his mind, will, and emotions) with all diligence, because his heart was the wellspring of life (v. 23). He told his son to cleanse himself of all ungodly and perverse speech (v. 24). He told his son to guard his eyes so that he would refrain from looking at things that would distract him (v. 25). He told his son to be careful where he went and to keep away from evil (vv. 26–27).

9. Answers will vary but can include the following: direct, specific, clear, concise, powerful, loving. Other answers can apply.

Study 3b   The Principal Thing

10. The son is instructed to acquire wise words by developing an aptitude for hearing them and recognizing their importance. He is also instructed to put away all forms of ungodly and perverse speech from his mind and mouth (Prov. 4:20–22, 24). Conversely, the immoral woman speaks words that are smoother than oil to the listener's ear, but they are deceitful. Her words eventually trap the listener and lead him to hell (Prov. 5:3–5).

11. The immoral woman's speech is convincing, but it is also dangerous (Prov. 5:3–5). She's an agent of the devil and leads those who follow her to hell (Prov. 5:5). Wise people stay far away from her because she traps victims (Prov. 5:8–9). She causes her victims to waste their lives and strength as they pursue empty words and covet her lustful charms (Prov. 5:9). She entices her victims by using her seductive physical beauty and promises them immoral sexual pleasure that has devastating consequences. This is a total lie (Prov. 5:20).

12. Paul said it was God's will that they refrain from all forms of sexual immorality (1 Thess. 4:3). He said they should learn to control their sexual appetites in a manner that is holy and honorable (1 Thess. 4:3–4). He said there should be a clear distinction between the sexual conduct of the unsaved and the saved (1 Thess. 4:5). He said they should not take advantage of other people sexually because God will punish them for these sins (1 Thess. 4:6). He said if they (the Thessalonian believers) reject what he wrote to them, then they were rejecting God, not him (1 Thess. 4:8).

13. a. The Bible teaches that homosexuality is a sin. It's a by-product of not honoring God as God and not being thankful (Rom. 1:21–23). When a person does not honor Him as God, He often allows them to begin a dangerous downward path that leads to mental confusion (Rom. 1:22) and idolatry (Rom. 1:23). If this happens and they're still unwilling to recognize their error, God often turns them over to the desires of their sinful hearts, which, for some, is expressed in homosexual behavior (Rom. 1:24–27). God continues to love them and wants them to return to their original created purpose of loving and honoring Him, but He withdraws His active pursuit of them so they might experience the wages of their iniquity and eventually repent. Homosexuality is a sin like any other expression of sin and can be repented of and forgiven by God. The apostle Paul, writing to the Corinthian believers, said that some of them had been homosexuals (1 Cor. 6:9–11). This passage is so specific that it identifies both the masculine and the feminine roles in a homosexual relationship (v. 9; homosexuals and sodomites). Paul makes a four-fold statement about these former homosexuals who are now Christians. He said, "Such were some of you, but you were washed, but you were sanctified, but you were justified" (1 Cor. 6:11). Some believers in the church had been homosexuals, but they were washed clean by the blood of Christ and the grace of God. They'd been set apart (sanctified) by God for His purposes. They had been saved and set free (justified), meaning they now had a proper legal standing before God. Perhaps the detailed description of this passage was meant to assure former homosexuals of God's forgiveness and remind the church that God fully embraced them as members of His family — something the church of Jesus Christ today would do well to consider.

   b. God's people need to educate themselves about the Bible's teaching on homosexuality, as well as its health effects. Parents should talk to educate their children on the moral and physical implications of all immoral conduct, including homosexuality. Other answers could apply.

14. a. Bitterness and death (Prov. 5:4–5). Financial ruin (Prov. 5:10). Sorrow (Prov. 5:11). Regret (Prov. 5:11–13). Dishonor among the body of Christ (Prov. 5:14).

   b. There are dozens of sexually transmitted diseases such as gonorrhea, syphilis, herpes, and AIDS. Many of these illnesses cause lifetime health-related problems, including sterility, pain, and even death. Some are incurable.

15. a. Rueben (Gen. 49:4). King David (2 Sam. 11:1–5). Amnon (2 Sam. 13:10–15).

   b. Stay away from them (Prov. 5:8). Don't lust after her beauty in your heart (Prov. 6:25).

16. Never stir up or arouse flames of passion (love) before a biblical opportunity for it to be satisfied. As the bride in the Song of Solomon experiences the burning flames of sexual passion, she realizes how powerful a force it is and warns the unmarried women in Jerusalem not to arouse their sexual appetites until they're married. This is good advice for all believers, young and old, men and women.

17. a. The man's wife. A cistern is a large reservoir in a home to hold rainwater. It could also refer to a large container (usually silver) used at the dining table for drinking water.

    b. A husband (or wife) should be sexually faithful to his spouse. His commitment to marital fidelity will prevent him from physical, emotional, and spiritual contamination.

18. Blessed, rejoice, enraptured (NIV – "captivated").

19. Satisfying sexual activity within the bonds of marriage is God's plan for husbands and wives. Familiarity does not necessarily and automatically lead to sexual boredom.

20. God watches every move Christians make, and He examines every step they take. Believers are not exempt from the temporal judgment of God when they engage in immoral behavior. If any man engages in sinful conduct, he will eventually become ensnared and may even die because of his lack of self-control and folly (Prov. 5:23).

Study 4a   How to Avoid Entrapment

1. a. As quickly as possible, the son was to get out of his commitment to put up security to the other man (Prov. 6:1–5).

    b. The gazelle is a fast runner, and this image conveys the speed by which the son was to escape from his folly. The use of the bird caught in a trap or snare likely meant the son should look for his first opportunity to escape and do so without looking back.

2. We're responsible to others and accountable to God for the words we speak and the commitments we make, even if those commitments are only verbal (Prov. 6:1–5). Believers should have no need to swear the things they say are true, because everything they say should be true (Matt. 5:33–37). The use and misuse of oaths to verify the things we say has its source in the devil himself (Matt. 5:37).

3. A believer should realize he has no control over the future, and his commitments to others should be in light of this important truth. When someone asks him to make a commitment he knows he might not fulfill, he should say, "If the Lord wills."

4. The ant works diligently without supervision (Prov. 6:7). The ant works diligently to prepare for times of future need (Prov. 6:8).

5. They have a tendency to rest or sleep when it's time to work (Prov. 6:9–10). Poverty comes upon them suddenly because of their indolence (Prov. 6:11).

6. a. He winks with his eyes (Prov. 6:13). This appears to refer to a signal between two people. in the presence of another who is being taken advantage of. He shuffles his feet and points with his fingers (Prov. 6:13). This tactic, often used by magicians to fool an audience, is a common tactic used by wicked people to confuse a person and communicate something other than what is said verbally.
    b. Calamity or disaster. They also face sudden destruction so severe they'll not be able to recover.

7. a. "A proud look, a lying tongue, hands that shed innocent blood, a heart that devises wicked plans, feet that are swift in running to evil, a false witness who speaks lies, one who sows discord among brethren."
    b. Answers will vary.

8. Evil. Seductress. Harlot. Adulteress.

9. a. God's people are commanded to flee immorality (1 Cor. 6:18). When an individual commits an act of immorality, he sins against God and his own body. His body, as the temple of the Holy Spirit, does not belong to him. His body belongs to God because it was purchased at the time of salvation by the blood of Jesus Christ. A believer is to glorify God in his body rather than using it to lustfully gratify the insatiable desires of the flesh (1 Cor. 6:19–20). The sexual unity of a married Christian couple is not to be defiled by introducing a third person into that blessed union (Heb. 13:4).
    b. Poverty (v. 26). Divine retribution (vv. 27–29). Damage to his soul (v. 32). Wounds (v. 33). Dishonor (v. 33). Enduring reproach (v. 33). Vengeance from the woman's husband (v. 34).

Study 4b How to Avoid Entrapment

10. Wisdom should become the apple of our eyes (v. 2). We should bind wisdom on our fingers and write wisdom on the tablet of our hearts (v. 3). We should say to wisdom (understanding), "You are my sister" (v. 4). We should call wisdom our nearest kin (v. 4).

11. a. 1. The father who looked through the window and observed a young man being trapped by an immoral woman (vv. 6–7).
    2. An unspecified number of young people, all apparently uncommitted to God or not desirous of following His ways (v. 7).
    3. A young man who lacked understanding was trapped by the adulteress (v. 8).
    4. An adulteress (v. 10).

    b. Answers will vary. This scene could possibly occur in bars, casinos, public beaches and lakes, resorts, cruise ships, office parties, work-related conventions and conferences, workout places. Other answers can apply.

12. a. 1. The young man lacked understanding (v. 7). He was a moral accident waiting to happen.
    2. He was unwise about where he went (v. 8).
    3. He was alone in a place where he could be easily tempted (v. 9). There's no mention of other young men attempting to discourage him from sin. He was unaccountable to anyone for his actions.

    b. 1. She is evil (Prov. 6:24). 2. She is an immoral woman who aggressively promotes her pagan lifestyle within the community through deceptive speech and suggestive enticements (Prov. 6:24–25). 3. She has a wicked heart and dresses like a harlot (Prov. 7:10). 4. She is loud and rebellious (Prov. 7:11). 5. She does not stay at home (Prov. 7:11–12). 6. She actively hunts for sexual victims (Prov. 7:13). 7. She is pretentious in her religious devotion (Prov. 7:14). 8. She is clamorous (Prov. 9:13). 9. She is overt in her immoral behavior (Prov. 9:14–17).

13. a. Answers will vary.
    b. The individual should be affirmed for his courage in sharing his problem with you. You should tell the individual the personal information he shared will not be shared with others — and mean it. Ask the individual what you can do to help him. Ask the individual how he sees the problem in relationship to God and His Word. You should consider meeting with him regularly for prayer, Bible study, and accountability. If you're not the right person to help him, consider introducing him to your pastor or another trustworthy Christian who can help

him gain victory over the problem. Believers should not counsel the opposite sex.

14. a. Lust is impatient, but love is patient (1 Cor. 13:4). Lust is often rude and boorish, but love is kind (1 Cor. 13:4). Lust flaunts itself and is proud of its sensuality, but love does not parade itself and is not arrogant (1 Cor. 13:4). Lust often expresses itself rudely, but love is not rude (1 Cor. 13:5). Lust focuses on human emotion and is often easily offended, but love is not easily provoked (1 Cor. 13:5). Lust seeks to take advantage of others, but love thinks no evil (1 Cor. 13:5). Lust endures little, but love bears and endures all things (1 Cor. 13:7).

   b. Answers will vary.

15. 1. "A fool to the correction of the stocks" (v. 22). 2. "As a bird hastens to the snare" (v. 23). "She has cast down many wounded" (v. 26). 4. "Her house is the way to hell" (v. 27). 5. "Descending to the chambers of death" (v. 27).

16. Christians can learn to stand for truth in all aspects of society. They can maintain sexual purity in their own lives and educate their children in the ways of the Lord, including God's sexual standards. They can vote for local, state, and national officials who support God's standard of moral behavior. They can voice their opinion in love at school board and other meetings. Other answers can apply.

Study 5a   The Excellence of Wisdom

1. a. Wisdom calls to anyone who will listen (vv. 2–3) but makes a special appeal to the simple and to fools (v. 5).
   b. The Word of God.
   c. 1. The believer must learn the Bible ("He who has My commandments"; John 14:21).
      2. The believer must obey the Bible ("and keeps them"; John 14:21).
      3. The believer must continue to pray to God for wisdom, trusting that He will answer his prayer (James 1:5–6).

2. "Excellent things" (v. 6). "Right things" (v. 6). "Truth" (v. 7). "Righteousness" (v. 8). "Plain" (v. 9). "Right" (v. 9). "Better than rubies" (v. 11). "All things ... cannot be compared with her" (v. 11).

3. Answers will vary but can include the following: 1) A believer should consider committing to study the Bible every day. 2) A believer should consider becoming an active part of a Bible-believing church where God's Word is taught accurately and lovingly. Other answers can apply.

4. Leaders need wisdom to help them listen carefully to understand others. Leaders are often tempted to "jump to conclusions" and then make decisions that harm others. Leaders need wisdom to think clearly so they make wise decisions that benefit their followers and maximize the skills and potential of those responsible to them. If a leader consistently makes unwise decisions, those who are following him will become frustrated and lose heart. Other answers can apply.

5. a. 1. God will demonstrate His abundant love to those who love Him (Prov. 8:17).
      2. If we diligently seek God, we will find Him (Prov. 8:17).
      3. If we ask for wisdom, God will give it to us generously (James 1:5).
   b. God will provide enduring riches, honor, righteousness, and divine fruit that is better than fine gold (vv. 18–19). God walks in the way of the righteous (a figure of speech to show that He observes what men do) to determine who is worthy to inherit wealth and have their treasuries filled (vv. 20–21). It's important to realize that financial blessing is not a guarantee to those who live according to His plan. Those who preach a "prosperity gospel" fail to realize that God chose many mighty saints (John the Baptist, Paul, the Macedonian believers) to be rich in faith and blessed in eternity (Heb. 11:36–39).

6. Believers should use the earth but not abuse it. It's a gift from God, and believers are commanded to be good stewards of the gifts God allows them to use.

7. a. The builder who built his house on the rock is compared to the man who builds his life on the Word of God. He hears and obeys the Word of God. When the winds of adversity come (rain, floods, winds), his life does not falter (Matt. 7:24–25). The builder who built his house on the sand is compared to a man who rejected the Word of God (he heard the Word but did not obey it) and lives by human reason. His life was shattered when adversity came.
   b. Only at times of adversity.

8. The Word of God did not help the Israelites during the Exodus because they were unwilling to trust God for what He said.

9. Answers will vary.

Study 5b   The Excellence of Wisdom

10. a. She invites the simple and the ones who lack understanding.
    b. She offers to serve them wisdom so they can live with understanding.

11. a. Connecting Proverb.

    b.   1.   Rebukes.

          2.   Wicked man.

          3.   Harms himself.

12. 1.   They do not want their sins to be exposed (John 3:19–20).

      2.   Satan has blinded the minds of all unsaved people. Only Christ can open their hearts and minds (2 Cor. 4:4).

13. a.   Their desires are contrary to God's will for their lives. Instead of yielding their hearts and minds to God, they reject the truth and find religious teachers who tell them what they want to hear rather than what they need to hear.

      b.   Timothy was to preach the Word of God at all times (v. 2). He was to do it with courage, concern, and patience (vv. 2, 5). He was to do it until God redirected his steps or removed him from the ministry, either by reassignment or death.

14. Answers will vary.

15. Answers will vary.

16. a.   Answers will vary. The fear of the Lord is reverential awe that causes a believer to put away all evil from his life and that motivates him to walk in God's ways, love Him, and serve Him with all his heart and soul.

      b.   Answers will vary.

      c.   Fear comes from the devil. The cure for fear is to acknowledge the abiding presence of the Lord (Isa. 41:10), knowing that He is our helper (Isa. 41:13). We must learn to actively wait on the Lord and trust Him to bring into our lives only what He divinely ordains for His glory. He created us, redeemed us, and He knows us intimately (Isa. 43:1). We can trust Him.

17. Answers will vary.

THE FINAL EXAM

Every person will eventually stand before God in judgment — the final exam. The Bible says, ***And it is appointed for men to die once, but after this comes judgment** (Heb. 9:27).*

May I ask you a question? *If you died today, do you know for certain you would go to heaven?* I did not ask if you're religious or a church member, nor did I ask if you've had some encounter with God — a meaningful, spiritual experience. I didn't even ask if you believe in God, or angels, or if you're trying to live a good life. The question I *am* asking is this: *If you died today, do you know for certain you would go to heaven?*

When you die, you will stand alone before God in judgment. You'll either be saved for all eternity, or you will be separated from God for all eternity in what the Bible calls the lake of fire (Rom. 14:12; Rev. 20:11–15). Tragically, many religious people who believe in God are not going to be accepted by Him when they die.

> ***"Many will say to Me in that day, 'Lord, Lord, have we not prophesied in Your name, cast out demons in Your name, and done many wonders in Your name?' And then I will declare to them, 'I never knew you; depart from Me, you who practice lawlessness!'"** (Matt 7:22–23).*

God loves you and wants you to go to heaven (John 3:16; 2 Peter 3:9). If you are not sure where you'll spend eternity, you are not prepared to meet God. God wants you to know for certain that you will go to heaven.

> ***Behold, now is the accepted time; behold, now is the day of salvation** (2 Cor. 6:2).*

The words ***behold*** and ***now*** are repeated because God wants you to know that you can be saved today. You do not need to hear those terrible words, ***Depart from Me....*** Isn't that great news?

Jesus himself said, ***You must be born again*** (John 3:7). These aren't the words of a pastor, a church, or a particular denomination. They're the words of Jesus Christ himself. You *must* be born again (saved from eternal damnation) before you die; otherwise, it will be too late when you die! You can know for certain today that God will accept you into heaven when you die.

> ***These things I have written to you who believe in the name of the Son of God, that you may <u>know</u> that you have eternal life** (1 John 5:13).*

The phrase ***you may know*** means that you can know for certain before you die that you will go to heaven. To be born again, you must understand and accept four essential spiritual truths. These truths are right from the Bible, so you know you can trust them — they are not man-made religious traditions. Now, let's consider these four essential spiritual truths.

FIRST ESSENTIAL SPIRITUAL TRUTH
THE BIBLE TEACHES THAT YOU ARE A SINNER AND SEPARATED FROM GOD.

No one is righteous in God's eyes. To be righteous means to be totally without sin, not even a single act.

> **There is none righteous, no, not one; There is none who understands; There is none who seeks after God. They have all turned aside; They have together become unprofitable; There is none who does good, no, not one** *(Rom. 3:10–12).*

> *...for all have sinned and fall short of the glory of God (Rom. 3:23).*

Look at the words God uses to show that all men are sinners — *none, not one, all turned aside, not one.* God is making a point — all men are sinners. No man is good (perfectly without sin) in His sight. The reason is sin.

Have you ever lied, lusted, hated someone, stolen anything, or taken God's name in vain, even once? These are all sins. Only one sin makes you a sinner and unrighteous in God's eyes.

Are you willing to admit to God that you are a sinner? If so, then tell Him right now you have sinned. You can say the words in your heart or aloud — it doesn't matter, but be honest with God. Now check the box if you have just admitted you are a sinner.

❑ *God, I admit I am a sinner in Your eyes.*

Now, let's look at the second essential spiritual truth.

SECOND ESSENTIAL SPIRITUAL TRUTH
THE BIBLE TEACHES THAT YOU CANNOT SAVE YOURSELF OR EARN YOUR WAY TO HEAVEN.

Man's sin is a very serious problem in the eyes of God. Your sin separates you from God, both now and for all eternity — unless you are born again.

> **For the wages of sin is death** *(Rom. 6:23).*

> **And you He made alive, who were dead in trespasses and sins** *(Eph. 2:1).*

Wages are a payment a person earns by what he or she has done. Your sin has earned you the wages of death, which means separation from God. If you die never having been born again, you will be separated from God after death.

You cannot save yourself or purchase your entrance into heaven. The Bible says that man is **not redeemed with corruptible things like gold or silver** (1 Peter 1:18). If you own all the money in the world, you cannot buy your entrance into heaven. Neither can you buy your way into heaven with good works.

> **For by grace you have been saved through faith, and that not of yourselves; it is the gift of God, not of works lest anyone should boast** (Eph. 2:8–9).

The Bible says salvation is **not of yourselves**. It is **not of works, lest anyone should boast.** Salvation from eternal judgment cannot be earned by doing good works — it is a gift of God. There is nothing you can do to purchase your way into heaven because you are already unrighteous in God's eyes.

If you understand you cannot save yourself, then tell God right now that you are a sinner, separated from Him, and you cannot save yourself. Check the box below if you have just done that.

❑ _God, I admit that I am separated from You because of my sin. I realize that I cannot save myself._

Now, let's look at the third essential spiritual truth.

THIRD ESSENTIAL SPIRITUAL TRUTH

THE BIBLE TEACHES THAT JESUS CHRIST DIED ON THE CROSS TO PAY THE COMPLETE PENALTY FOR YOUR SIN AND TO PURCHASE A PLACE IN HEAVEN FOR YOU.

Jesus Christ, the sinless Son of God, lived a perfect life, died on the cross, and rose from the dead to pay the penalty for your sin and purchase a place in heaven for you. He died on the cross on your behalf, in your place, as your substitute, so you do not have to go to hell. Jesus Christ is the only acceptable substitute for your sin.

> **For He [God, the Father] made Him [Jesus] who knew [committed] no sin to be sin for us, that we might become the righteousness of God in Him** (2 Cor. 5:21).

> **I [Jesus] am the way, the truth, and the life. No one comes to the Father except through Me** (John 14:6).

> **Nor is there salvation in any other, for there is no other name under heaven given among men by which we must be saved.** (Acts 4:12).

Jesus Christ is your only hope and means of salvation. Because you are a sinner, you cannot pay for your sins, but Jesus paid the penalty for your sins by dying on the cross in your place. Friend, there is salvation in no one else — not angels, not some religious leader, not even your religious good works. No religious act such as baptism, confirmation, or joining a church can save you. There is no other way, no other name that can save you. Only Jesus Christ can save you. You must be saved by accepting Jesus Christ's substitutionary sacrifice for your sins, or you will be lost forever.

Do you see clearly that Jesus Christ is the only way to God in heaven? If you understand this truth, tell God that you understand, and check the box below.

❏ *God, I understand that Jesus Christ died to pay the penalty for my sin. I understand that His death on the cross was the only acceptable sacrifice for my sin.*

FOURTH ESSENTIAL SPIRITUAL TRUTH
BY FAITH, YOU MUST TRUST IN JESUS CHRIST ALONE FOR ETERNAL LIFE AND CALL UPON HIM TO BE YOUR SAVIOR AND LORD.

Many religious people admit they have sinned. They believe Jesus Christ died for the sins of the world but they are not saved. Why? Thousands of moral, religious people have never completely placed their faith in Jesus Christ *alone* for eternal life. They think they must believe in Jesus Christ as a real person and do good works to earn their way to heaven. They are not trusting Jesus Christ alone. To be saved, you must trust in Jesus Christ *alone* for eternal life. Look what the Bible teaches about trusting Jesus Christ alone for salvation.

> **_Believe_ on the Lord Jesus Christ, and you will be saved** (Acts 16:31).

> **...that if you confess with your mouth the Lord Jesus and _believe_ in your heart that God has raised Him from the dead, you will be saved. For with the heart one believes unto righteousness, and with the mouth confession is made unto salvation. For there is no distinction between Jew and Greek, for the same Lord over all is rich to all who call upon Him. For "Whoever calls on the name of the LORD shall be saved** (Rom. 10:9–10, 12–13).

Do you see what God is saying? To be saved or born again, you must trust Jesus Christ *alone* for eternal life. Jesus Christ paid for your complete salvation. Jesus said, **It is finished** (John 19:30). Jesus paid for your salvation completely when He shed His blood on the cross for your sin.

If you believe that God resurrected Jesus Christ (proving God's acceptance of Jesus as a worthy sacrifice for man's sin) and you are willing to confess Jesus Christ as your Savior and Lord (master of your life), you will be saved.

Friend, right now God is offering you the greatest gift in the world. God wants to give you the *gift* of eternal life, the *gift* of His complete forgiveness for all your sins, and the *gift* of His unconditional acceptance into heaven when you die. Will you accept His free gift now, right where you are?

Are you unsure how to receive the gift of eternal life? Let me help you. Do you remember that I said you needed to understand and accept four essential spiritual truths? First, you admitted you are a sinner. Second, you admitted you were separated from God because of your sin and you could not save yourself. Third, you realized that Jesus Christ is the only way to heaven — no other name can save you.

Now, you must trust that Jesus Christ once and for all to save your lost soul. Just take God at His word — He will not lie to you! This is the kind of simple faith you need to be saved. If you would like to be saved right now, right where you are, offer this prayer of simple faith to God. Remember, the words must come from your heart.

> *God, I am a sinner and deserve to go to hell. Thank you Jesus for dying on the cross for me and for purchasing a place in heaven for me. I believe you are the Son of God and you are able to save me right now. Please forgive me for my sin and take me to heaven when I die. I invite you into my life as Savior and Lord and I trust you alone for eternal life. Thank you for giving me the gift of eternal life. Amen.*

If, in the best way you know how, you trusted Jesus Christ alone to save you, then God just saved you. He said in His Holy Word, *But as many as received Him, to them He gave the right to become the children of God.* (John 1:12). It's that simple. God just gave you the gift of eternal life by faith. You have just been born again according to the Bible.

You will not come into eternal judgment, and you will not perish in the lake of fire — you are saved forever! Read this verse carefully and let it sink into your heart.

> *Most assuredly, I say to you, he who hears My word and believes in Him who sent Me has everlasting life, and shall not come into judgment, but has passed from death into life (John 5:24).*

Now, let me ask you a few more questions.

According to God's Holy Word (John 5:24), not your feelings, what kind of life did God just give you? _____ What two words did God say at the beginning of the verse to assure you that He is not lying to you? _____ _____ Are you going to come into judgment? YES or NO _____. Have you passed from spiritual death into life? YES or NO _____ .

Friend, you've just been born again. You just became a child of God.

We'd like to help you grow in your new Christian life. We will send you a Spiritual Birth Certificate to remind you of your spiritual birthday and some Bible study materials to help you understand more about the Christian life. To receive these helpful materials free of charge, photocopy the form below, fill it out, and send it to us by mail, or you can e-mail your request to: resources@LamplightersUSA.org.

Lamplighters Response Card

❑ I just accepted Jesus Christ as my Savior and Lord on (date) _____, 200____
    at _____.

❑ Please send me the Spiritual Birth Certificate and Bible study materials to help me
    grow as a Christian.

❑ I would like to begin attending a Bible-believing church. Please recommend some
    Bible-believing churches in the area where I live.

❑ I already know of a good Bible-believing church that I will be attending to help me
    grow as a new Christian.

Name _____

Address _____

City _____ State _____ Zip _____

E-mail Address_____

To purchase additional Lamplighters Bible Study resources contact:

Lamplighters International,
6301 Wayzata Blvd, St. Louis Park, Minnesota 55416, USA.

Or call 800 507-9516

Or visit our website at: www.LamplightersUSA.org